Scooter

KERRI MAZZARELLA

Table of Contents

A Pelican Book

Teaching Tips for Caregivers and Teachers:

Research shows that one of the best ways for students to learn a new topic is to read about it.

Before Reading

- Read the title and predict what the book will be about.
- Read the "Words to Know" and discuss the meaning of each word.
- Read the back cover to see what the book is about.

During Reading

- When a student gets to a word that is unknown, ask them to look at the rest of the sentence to find clues to help with the meaning of the unknown word.
- Motivate students with praise and encouragement.

After Reading

- Discuss the main idea of the book.
- Ask students to give one detail that they learned in the book.

SIGHT WORDS

a	has	on	use
and	I	ride	with
for	is	the	
fun	my	this	

Words to Know

friends

helmet

pads

scooter

sidewalk

wheels

This is my **scooter**.

My scooter has **wheels**.

I use a **helmet** and **pads**.

I ride my scooter
on the **sidewalk**.

I ride my scooter
with **friends**.

I ride my scooter for fun!

Index

Written by: Kerri Mazzarella
Design by: Jen Bowers
Series Development: James Earley

Photos: Shutterstock.com/cover & p.3, 10, 11 ©2018 Monkey Business Images, cover & interior sports icons ©Geanine87; p.3 & 12 ©2021 HelgaPhoto.ru; p.3 & 9 ©2022 Troyan; p.3 & 5 ©2020 AnnaMedia; p.3 & 7 ©2017 Dzha33; p.4 ©2020 Fab_1; p.6 ©2022 Sergey Ryzhov; p.8 ©2010 Evgenia Sh.; p.13 ©2021 Olena Gaidarzhy; p.14 ©2016 FamVeld; p.15 ©2018 Monkey Business Images

Library of Congress PCN Data
Scooter / Kerri Mazzarella
My 1st
ISBN 979-8-8873-5327-2 (hard cover)
ISBN 979-8-8873-5412-5 (paperback)
ISBN 979-8-8873-5497-2 (EPUB)
ISBN 979-8-8873-5582-5 (eBook)
Library of Congress Control Number: 2022948429
Printed in the United States of America.

Seahorse Publishing Company
www.seahorsepub.com

Published in the United States
Seahorse Publishing
PO Box 771325
Coral Springs, FL 33077